explore

ok 1

Discipleship Series

Uncover the Truth about God

Student Book

wph wesleyan publishing house

Indianapolis, Indiana

Uncover the Truth about God
Student Book 1 in the Explore Kid's Discipleship Series

Published by Wesleyan Publishing House
Indianapolis, Indiana 46250
Printed in the United States of America
ISBN: 978-0-89827-411-0

Contributors
Executive Editor: Colleen Derr
Authors: Angie Young and Andrew Bush
Art Director/Designer: Kory Pence
Illustrator: Daniel Swartz

book 1 explore

www.wesleyan.org/wph

contents

explore | Uncover the Truth about God

God

We can believe in God even though we can't see Him.

Engage

There are so many things that we believe in even though we can't see them. We believe in gravity, wind, and air. We believe in these things because we can see the effects they have on the world around us. Just like each of these things, we can believe in God because we can see the effects that He has had on nature, in Scripture, and throughout history.

I Can Know It Is True

1. We can see the effects God has on nature. Nature didn't happen by accident. Nature is creative and organized. Nature points us towards an intelligent creator, God.

   We can read about the effects God has on nature in Genesis 1:1—2:4 and Isaiah 44:24.

2. We can see the effects God has in Scripture. Even though humans wrote the Bible, God inspired each word.

   We can read about the effects God has in Scripture in 2 Timothy 3:16.

3. We can see the effects God has throughout history. History has been affected by the many miracles that God has performed. God still performs miracles and is changing lives everyday!

   We can read about the effect God has throughout history in Exodus 4:1–17; Daniel 6; and Acts 16:16–34.

Even though you may not be able to physically see God today, He reveals himself to you through nature, Scripture, and history. Take a look around and begin to discover what an amazing and powerful God we worship!

Check It Out

Read Romans 1:20.

What are some of God's invisible qualities that are revealed in nature?

Read Matthew 22:29.

How is the power of God shown in Scripture?

Read Job 5:9 and Deuteronomy 10:21.

What can we learn about God through the miracles He performs?

Question

Read Job 38:1–12.

What verse sticks out to you? Why?

Nature is full of amazing and complex things. Think about the sun. If it were located any closer to the earth, we would not be able to survive because of the intense heat. If it were located any farther from the earth, we would not be able to survive because of the extreme cold. God knew how large the sun needed to be, exactly where it needed to be located, and how fast the earth needed to rotate around it in order for us to live here on earth. Creation is no accident.

Think about the world around you. What are four other parts of creation that you think are too complex to be an accident?

1.
2.
3.
4.

Take a moment and thank God for creating each of those things.

Psalm 106:2 says, "Who can list the glorious miracles of the LORD? Who can ever praise him enough?"

See how many miracles you can list in three minutes!

Deuteronomy 4:32 says. "Now search all of history, from the time God created people on the earth until now, and search from one end of the heavens to the other. Has anything as great as this ever been seen or heard before?"

In this passage, God was challenging the Israelites to look at their history and remember what God had done for them.

Think about your life. List two or three things that God has done for you.

Challenge

As you *Explore* through the week, your challenge is to uncover five different ways God is at work around you. Make a list of the effects of God that you see and hear this week.

At the end of each day, take time to praise God for each one you have written down.

Don't forget to bring your list to class next week so we can share what we've seen and heard.

1.
2.
3.
4.
5.

Explore

Romans 1:20 says, "For ever since the world was created, people have seen the earth and sky. Through everything God made, they can clearly see his invisible qualities—his external power and divine nature. So they have no excuse for not knowing God."

Sign your name below if you accept the challenge to learn this verse in just one week.

X ....

The Bible

God's Word is our instruction book for life.

Engage

God's Word, the Bible, is like a recipe for our lives. The Bible gives you instructions on how to live. Just like there are things you need to understand when making a recipe, the Bible has three truths that you need to know in order to understand and trust it. Take a closer look at what God's Word is all about.

I Can Know It Is True

1. God's Word is true. As we read the Bible, we can be sure that we are reading the truth. There is not one verse in the Bible that is false. God means what He says in the Bible, and we can trust in Him to keep His promises.

   Check out what it says in Proverbs 30:5 and James 1:18.

2. God's Word teaches us who God is. God loves us and wants us to know Him. All throughout the Bible, God shows us who He is and how to have a friendship with Him.

   You can learn more about who God is in Isaiah 44:8; Jeremiah 23:24; and Matthew 5:48.

3. God's Word helps us know right from wrong. Life is full of decisions. We may not always know which way to go. The Bible helps us to learn which choices are right and which choices are wrong.

   Read about it in Psalm 1:1–2; Romans 2:18; and James 1:22–25.

   The Bible gives us instructions on how to have the best life possible.

Check It Out

Read Psalm 33:4 and 2 Timothy 3:14.
Why is it important to know that God's Word is true?

Read Psalm 90:2; Jeremiah 32:17; and Ephesians 2:18.
What do these verses say about who God is?

Read 2 Timothy 3:16–17.
What is one thing the Bible tells you *not* to do? What is one thing the Bible says that you *should* do?

Question

How is trying to live life without reading the Bible like trying to make cookies without using a recipe?

We all know that God's Word is important. Yet many of us don't take time everyday to read what God has to say to us.

What are three things that keep you from reading the Bible?

1.
2.
3.

What are some ways you can overcome those things?

God loves you and wants you to know Him. That's why He gave His Word. The Bible is God's letter of friendship and love sent just for you. Make it a habit to take some time during your day to let God talk to you through His Word, the Bible.

Challenge

This week uncover the truth about God in Mark 8.

As you read the chapter, use a pencil to underline anything that you don't understand. Circle the Scripture that says who Jesus is.

Reading Plan

Monday

Mark 8:1–10, "Jesus Feeds Four Thousand"

Tuesday

Mark 8:11–13, "Pharisees Demand a Miraculous Sign"

Wednesday

Mark 8:14–21, "Yeast of the Pharisees and Herod"

Thursday

Mark 8:22–26, "Jesus Heals a Blind Man"

Friday

Mark 8:27–30, "Peter's Declaration about Jesus"

Saturday

Mark 8:31–38, "Jesus Predicts His Death"

Explore

Second Timothy 3:16–17 says, "All Scripture is inspired by God and is useful to teach us what is true and to make us realize what is wrong in our lives. It corrects us when we are wrong and teaches us to do what is right. God uses it to prepare and equip his people to do every good work."

Repeat the *Explore* verse every day before you begin your reading in Mark.

Sin

We have all sinned and there are consequences that come with sin.

Engage

No matter how hard you stir them, water and oil won't mix; they remain separate. There is something in our life that separates us from having a relationship with God. That thing is called *sin*.

We have all sinned and there are consequences that come with sin.

I Can Know It Is True

1. Because of Adam and Eve, we are all born into sin. Adam and Eve were created by God to live forever in a perfect place called the Garden of Eden. The only rule they were given was to not eat from one tree, the Tree of Knowledge of Good and Evil. When faced with temptation, though, they gave in and ate the forbidden fruit. They sinned. This act of sin resulted in some serious consequences. These consequences don't just apply to Adam and Eve. They apply to us all.

   Read the story of Adam and Eve to discover the consequences of their sin. Look in Genesis 2:15–17; Genesis 3; and Romans 5:12–19.

2. Sin is willful disobedience against God and can be an action or an attitude. It's easy to read the story of Adam and Eve and think that if we had been in their place we wouldn't have messed up like they did. But the Bible says that we have all sinned. At some point in our lives we have all chosen to disobey God. Sometimes we disobey God through our actions like lying, stealing, or cheating. Other times we disobey Him through our attitudes like being disrespectful, holding grudges against someone, or choosing not to love another person.

   See what the Bible says about sin in 1 John 3:4; James 4:17; and Matthew 5:21–22.

3. Sin separates us from God, but He provided the way to make us right with Him again. God sent His Son Jesus to pay the price for our sin so we could once again have a relationship with Him!

   Discover God's plan for us to become re-connected with Him in John 3:16; Galatians 1:4; and Hebrews 9:27–28.

   We have all sinned. Sin comes with consequences. Sometimes the consequence of our sin is being punished or disciplined. The biggest consequence of our sin is a broken relationship with God. But God has made a way for us to once again have a relationship with Him!

Check It Out

Read 1 Corinthians 15:21–22.

What is this verse saying? Why do you think we all have to pay for Adam's and Eve's sin?

Read Romans 3:23.

How do you define sin? What do you think God's glorious standard is?

Read Romans 6:23.

This verse says that one of the wages (consequences) of sin is death. What are some of the other consequences of sin?

Question

On a scale of one to ten, one being easy and ten being hard, how hard do you think it would have been to NOT eat from the Tree of the Knowledge of Good and Evil? Why?

You might think that you would have been able to avoid making the same mistake Adam and Eve did. But we're all human which means we all sin. We've all given into temptation.

What is the difference between making a mistake and sinning?

Sin is willful disobedience against God. It is choosing to do something even though you know it is wrong. The verse following has a long list of sins.

Circle every sin that is an action sin and underline each sin that would be considered an attitude sin.

"Their lives became full of every kind of wickedness, sin, greed, hate, envy, murder, quarreling, deception, malicious behavior, and gossip. They are backstabbers, haters of God, insolent, proud, and boastful. They invent new ways of sinning, and they disobey their parents" (Rom. 1:29–30).

Some people make the mistake of thinking that if you simply attend church every once in awhile, you can have a relationship with God. What are some other things people think they can do to earn a relationship with God?

John 14:6 says, "Jesus told him, I am the way, the truth, and the life. No one can come to the Father except through me."

This verse reminds us that there is only one way to have a relationship with God and that is through Jesus Christ.

Challenge

This week, think about your relationship with God and write down three sins that you have committed or struggled with. Then list the consequences that you have had to face because of those sins. Take time to reflect on what you have learned from each incident. You will not be required to share what you wrote next week if you do not want to.

	Sin	Consequence	What I've Learned
1.			
2.			
3.			

Explore

John 3:16–17 says, "For God loved the world so much that he gave his one and only Son, so that everyone who believes in him will not perish but have eternal life. God sent his Son into the world not to judge the world, but to save the world through him."

Think about what those verses mean. Write down your thoughts.

Jesus

Jesus paid the permanent price for our sins.

Engage

Sometimes making sacrifices can be hard, especially when we're sacrificing something that we love. Jesus made the ultimate sacrifice for us. He sacrificed more than a candy bar or a video game. Jesus sacrificed His life for us.

Jesus paid the permanent price for our sins.

I Can Know It Is True

1. God requires atonement or payment for our sins. The Bible says that the payment for sin is death. That's a big price to pay.

   We read about the payment God requires for our sins in Romans 6:23 and 1 Corinthians 15:21–22.

2. In the Old Testament, sacrifices were required to gain forgiveness for sins. These sacrifices were temporary so people had to keep making sacrifices in order to remain in a right relationship with God.

   We can read about what the Bible has to say about Old Testament sacrifices in Leviticus 4:1–2, 32–35; Hebrews 9:22; and Hebrews 10:1.

3. Jesus was our perfect sacrifice and paid the permanent price for our sins. After a while, the sacrifice system in the Old Testament started to become nothing more than a meaningless routine. God knew people needed something different, something that would really change their lives. So God sent Jesus to pay the permanent price for our sins. Jesus came to earth and lived a perfect life, a life with no sin, and then died for our sins.

   See what the Bible says about Jesus and the perfect sacrifice He made for us in Galatians 1:4; Hebrews 10:12; and 1 Peter 2:22–23.

   Jesus made the ultimate sacrifice for us. He gave His life to help make a way for us to have eternal life in heaven with God. Jesus paid the permanent price for our sins.

Check It Out

Read Hebrews 4:15.

What kind of temptations do you think Jesus faced?

Read 1 John 2:2 and Hebrews 10:10.

What do these verses tell you about the sacrifice that Jesus made?

Question

Why does God require payment for sin?

When you get in trouble for doing something wrong, do you often complain that the punishment is unfair or unjust? Do you think that God was unfair or unjust to require death as a payment for sin? Why or why not.

Check out what Romans 3:23–26 says. Do these verses change your answer?

Jesus was faced with the same temptations that you face. In fact, He was even tempted by Satan himself. The Bible says that Jesus resisted temptation in every situation He faced. Jesus lived a perfect life, a life without sin.

Why is it important to know that Jesus lived a perfect life?

Jesus' sacrifice provides forgiveness for our sins. What else does Jesus' sacrifice provide for you?

Jesus sacrificed His life for all people for all time. What kind of sacrifices can you make that would please God?

For some help, check out these verses: Romans 12:1 and Hebrews 13:15–16.

Challenge

This week, your assignment is to practice sacrificial living. Choose to give up one thing you like for a whole week. It can be a favorite TV show, video games, favorite snack, or anything else that will be hard to live without. Every time you think about the thing you are giving up, take a moment to thank Jesus for His ultimate sacrifice.

In the space below, write what you plan to give up. Then ask a friend to sign as your witness.

Item I am giving up:

Friend's Signature:

X ....

Explore

Romans 3:23 and 6:23 say, "For everyone has sinned; we all fall short of God's glorious standard . . . For the wages of sin is death, but the free gift of God is eternal life through Christ Jesus our Lord."

Every time you are tempted to eat or do whatever you have sacrificed, say these verses out loud. By the end of the week you'll have them memorized.

Salvation

Because God loves us, He sent Jesus to pay the price for our sins.

Engage

God loves us so much that He sent His son Jesus to earth to live a perfect life, to die on the cross to pay the price for our sins, and to rise again from the dead.

I Can Know It Is True

1. To accept this gift of forgiveness, we must confess that we're sinners. Admitting that you have sinned is more than just saying you're sorry. It's asking God to forgive you for the sins you have committed and then, with God's help, to turn away and not do them again.

   See what the Bible says about finding God's forgiveness when we admit our sins in Romans 3:23; Acts 3:19; and 1 John 1:8–9.

2. To accept this gift of forgiveness, we must believe in Jesus. We must believe that Jesus is the son of God, lived a perfect life, died for our sins, and was raised from the dead three days later. Finally, we must believe Jesus is the *only* way we can have a relationship with God.

   We can read about the importance of believing in Jesus in John 3:16 and Galatians 3:22.

3. To accept this gift of forgiveness, we must commit our lives to God. We need to strive to become more like Christ.

   See what the Bible says about becoming more Christ-like in Ephesians 4:21–23 and Ephesians 5:1–2.

Check It Out

Read John 14:6.
Why is it important for you to believe that Jesus is the only way to have a relationship with God?

Read Romans 3:22.
Is it reassuring to know that anyone who believes can find forgiveness? Why or why not?

Because God loves you, He sent Jesus to pay the price for your sins. Whenever you're ready to accept God's gift of forgiveness, all you have to do is talk to Him and confess your sins, believe in what Jesus has done for you, and accept Him as your Savior.

Question

God made a way for us to restore our relationship with Him by sending Jesus to pay the price for our sins. How does this prove God's love for you?

Everyone loves receiving and accepting gifts. Do you think accepting God's gift of forgiveness is as easy as accepting a birthday gift? Why or why not?

Asking for forgiveness is sometimes called *becoming saved*. Why do you think it is called that?

What are some other terms that you've heard?

Do these terms make sense or are they confusing?

Have you accepted the gift of forgiveness?

If yes, who are some people that helped you make this decision?

If not, who are some people you could go to if you had questions about finding God's forgiveness?

If you haven't accepted this gift of forgiveness and you would like to, today is a great day to do it. Talk to your parents, pastor, or youth leader.

Challenge

This week, journal about when you accepted Christ as your Savior. Write out how you came to admit your sins, believe in Jesus, and commit your life to God.

If you have not accepted Jesus as your Savior, journal about what is holding you back.

When you are done with your journal, share what you have written with a parent, a caregiver, or an adult that you trust.

My Salvation Journey

X ....

Explore

John 14:6 says, "Jesus told him, "I am the way, the truth, and the life. No one can come to the Father except through me."

Say this verse each morning and evening, so that it will be sealed in your heart and mind.

Baptism

Baptism shows others what happened when you accepted Jesus as your Savior.

Engage

Romans 6:4

"For we died and were buried with Christ by baptism. And just as Christ was raised from the dead by the glorious power of the Father, now we also may live new lives."

I Can Know It Is True

1. Baptism symbolizes Jesus washing away our sins. When you ask Jesus to forgive you for all your sins, He removes them completely. He washes them away, and you become pure and clean in God's eyes. Baptism helps others to see on the outside the change that Jesus has made on the inside.

   We read how Jesus washes our sins away in Psalm 51:7 and 1 Peter 3:21.

2. Baptism symbolizes Jesus' death and resurrection. Jesus died for our sins, was buried in a tomb, and rose from the dead three days later. Not only did Jesus die to pay the price for our sins, but He also conquered death. Baptism is a representation of Jesus' death and resurrection.

   Discover how baptism symbolizes Jesus' death and resurrection in Romans 6:5–11 and Romans 6:3–4.

3. Baptism is a public statement of our faith. Once we have accepted Jesus as our forever friend we don't want to keep this news to ourselves. Baptism shows other people that you love God and have made the decision to follow Him.

   See what the Bible says in Acts 22:15–16 and Galatians 3:27.

Check It Out

Read Titus 3:4–5.

These verses remind us that we could not find salvation through our own good works but only through the mercy of God. How can baptism be a way of giving back to God for all the mercy He has shown you?

Read Colossians 2:12.

How does baptism visually represent the death and resurrection of Jesus Christ?

Question

After all you have learned, what do you think are the requirements for baptism?

Baptism gives your family and friends the opportunity to see on the outside the decision you made on the inside when you accepted Jesus as your Savior. It's a time of sharing and celebration.

List five to ten people you would invite to your baptism.

1.
2.
3.
4.
5.

People are usually given the opportunity to share a few words before they are baptized. Why do you think people are given this opportunity?

You can read about the baptism of Jesus in Matthew 3. Why do you think Jesus took the time to be baptized?

When Jesus was baptized He set an example for us. How can your baptism set an example for the people around you?

Are you ready to be baptized?

If yes, explain why you would like to be baptized.

If no, list one or two questions you still have about baptism.

Challenge

As you *Explore* this week, fill out "What God Has Done for Me!" on the next page.

Next, decide if you are ready for baptism. Take time to pray and talk with your parents or caregivers and pastor. If you are ready to be baptized, let them know! If you are not ready, write down what is keeping you from taking that step.

Explore

Titus 3:4–5 says, "But—'When God our Savior revealed his kindness and love, he saved us, not because of the righteous things we had done, but because of his mercy. He washed away our sins, giving us a new birth and new life through the Holy Spirit.'"

Learn these verses so you can share them at your baptism!

What God Has Done for Me!

Why I am ready to be baptized:

My parents or caregivers agree:

Or, I am not ready to be baptized and here is why:

1.
2.

My Baptism Celebration

Date:

Location:

I was baptized by:

My baptism memory:

Congratulations

on the steps you have taken to uncover the truth about God.

Your challenge is to continue to *Explore* as you discover your place in God's plan!